Cambridge Rea'ing Club

Le

Serie.

Q4

A Puzzle for Logan

Richard MacAndrew

GRUPO sm

CAMBRIDGE
UNIVERSITY PRESS

PUBLISHED BY THE PRESS SYNDICATE OF THE UNIVERSITY OF CAMBRIDGE
The Pitt Building, Trumpington Street, Cambridge, United Kingdom

CAMBRIDGE UNIVERSITY PRESS
The Edinburgh Building, Cambridge CB2 2RU, UK
40 West 20th Street, New York, NY 10011-4211, USA
477 Williamstown Road, Port Melbourne, VIC 3207, Australia
Ruiz de Alarcón 13, 28014 Madrid, Spain
Dock House, The Waterfront, Cape Town 8001, South Africa

http://www.cambridge.org

First published 2001
First published under Cambridge Reading Club 2004

Printed in Spain by Cayfosa Quebecor

Typeset in 12/15pt Adobe Garamond [CE]

For Cathy

Contents

Characters

Inspector Jenny Logan: a police officer in Edinburgh.
Sergeant Grant: an officer helping Inspector Logan.
Ronnie Campbell: in prison for murder.
Helen Robertson: a police doctor.
Jimmy Brown: a criminal.
Morag Mackenzie: Jimmy Brown's girlfriend.
Craig Sinclair: murdered seven years ago.
Jean Drummond: Craig Sinclair's sister.
Robert Baxter: a business man.
Angus (Gus) MacLeod: a homeless man.
Tam MacDonald: a journalist.

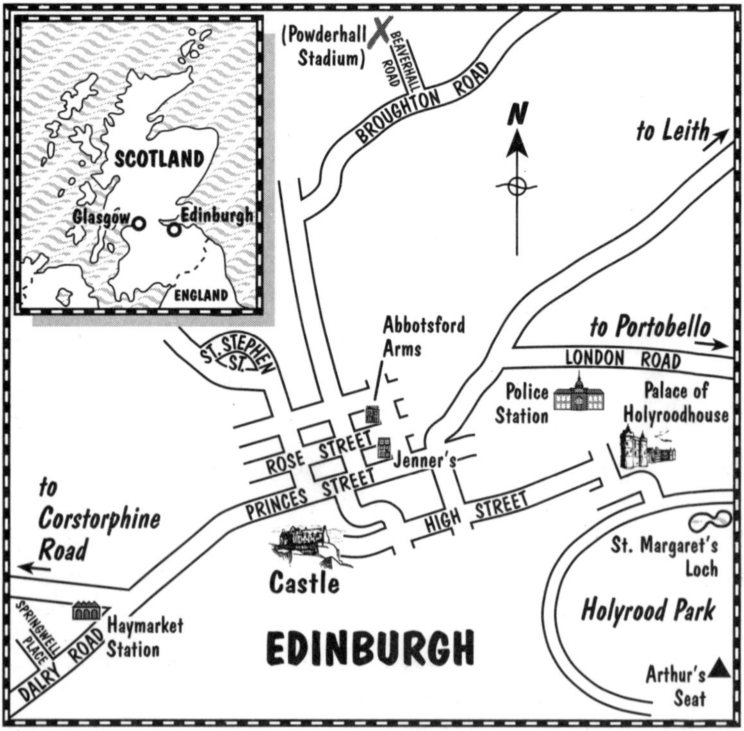

Chapter 1 *An escape and a murder*

Jenny Logan was enjoying an afternoon of warm Scottish sunshine on the beach at Portobello, five kilometres from the centre of Edinburgh, when her phone rang.

'Logan.'

'Grant here, madam.'

'It's my day off, Grant,' said Logan.

'I know. I'm sorry,' said Grant. 'But Ronnie Campbell, the murderer, has escaped from prison.'

'OK,' said Logan. 'I'll meet you in my office in about fifteen minutes.'

She put on jeans and a T-shirt over her swimsuit and walked quickly to her car.

* * *

Jenny Logan was an inspector in the Edinburgh Police. During the ten-minute drive from Portobello to the London Road police station, she thought about Ronnie Campbell. She knew that he had gone to prison for murdering a man called Craig Sinclair. That was about seven years ago, just after she had joined the police, but she couldn't remember anything else.

Sergeant Grant was waiting for Logan in her office. He was fifty-nine but looked younger. His hair was thick and black and he had a large black moustache. He was holding some papers with 'Police Record: Ronnie Campbell' written on the front.

'Tell me what's happening,' said Logan, putting her beach bag in a cupboard under the window.

'Campbell escaped from a prison van near Dundee some time this morning,' said Grant. 'They were moving him down to Saughton.' Saughton was a prison in the western part of Edinburgh. 'Campbell escaped at a petrol station and got away. We found out later he'd stolen a car, a dark blue Audi.'

'What have you done so far?' asked Logan.

'We've told the newspapers, the radio and the TV stations. We've given them the car number, and described what Campbell was wearing.'

Logan said nothing and thought for a moment.

'Is he dangerous, do you think?' she asked Grant.

'Possibly,' said Grant, putting Campbell's police record on Logan's desk and pointing to it. He opened his mouth to say something else but just then the phone rang. Grant answered it. He listened, said OK twice and then put the phone down. He looked at Logan.

'Someone's found a young woman's body in Holyrood Park. We're wanted over there immediately.'

'Today was my day off,' said Logan.

'Not any longer!' said Grant.

A few minutes later, Logan, with Grant beside her in the car, entered Holyrood Park. Holyrood Park is one of the most beautiful places in Edinburgh. Inside the park is Arthur's Seat, the tall hill that stands over all of Edinburgh. There are also lakes and fields. What other capital city in the world has such a large area of wild, green and open land so close to its centre? Edinburgh people know it well and love it; tourists do not often go there.

As she drove past the Palace of Holyroodhouse, the Queen's palace in Scotland, Logan remembered that in the middle of the sixteenth century there had been a very bloody murder inside the palace itself. She asked herself what they would find as she reached the group of police cars.

Logan parked her car on the grass at the side of the road behind the last police car. She got out and looked up at Arthur's Seat. The sky was blue and it was still warm, but Logan began to feel cold at the unfairness of a young woman's early death.

There was a group of people, almost all men, standing about a hundred metres away on the hillside. Logan and Grant walked up the hill towards the group. When they arrived, people moved back to let them through. Logan stepped forward and looked down at the body of a young woman in her late twenties. There was a wide cut across the woman's throat and blood everywhere. A dark-haired woman in blue trousers and a white shirt was studying the body carefully. This woman was Helen Robertson, the police doctor. Logan had met her a few times.

'Helen,' said Logan softly.

Robertson looked up.

'Jenny,' she said. 'Hi. A bad business, I'm afraid.' She turned back to the body but went on talking. 'As you can see, someone cut her throat with a knife. It's almost cut her head away from her body and there's a lot of blood.' She pointed at the ground near the body.

'Time of death . . . Probably between two and three this afternoon.'

Robertson continued to move round the body. She touched it as little as possible, only when she needed to see something better.

'I can't be sure until I've carefully . . .' She stopped as she looked more closely at something.

'Yes?' said Logan.

'Well, look at how the cut starts at the bottom of the neck here on the right and finishes close to her left ear. I would say the killer stood behind her and held her head back with his right arm. Then he cut her throat, holding the knife in his left hand.'

'I see,' said Logan. 'How sure are you?'

'Sure enough,' said Robertson, looking up with a serious smile on her face. 'And I'd also say he, or she, is quite a bit taller than this woman.' She nodded her head at the body on the ground in front of her. 'And this woman's actually quite tall herself. I'd say about 165, 170 centimetres.'

'Thanks, Helen,' said Logan. 'If there's anything else . . .'

'I'll let you know,' finished Robertson. 'There is one other thing. The killer will probably have blood all over his clothes.'

'OK. That's useful.' Logan turned to Grant. 'We need to find the knife, if possible,' she said. 'Get some people to search the park.'

'Right, madam,' said Grant.

Logan looked at her watch. It was only five o'clock. It would be light for a long time yet. 'The park's a big place but they can look till it gets dark,' she said. 'They've probably got another four or five hours at least.'

Grant moved away and started giving orders to some of

the police officers standing around. Logan walked some metres away from the body and allowed the sunshine and fresh air to take away some of the coldness of death.

A few minutes later, Grant came back towards Logan with Helen Robertson.

'I found this in her pocket,' said Robertson, passing Logan a clear plastic police bag with a rather dirty envelope inside it.

Logan took the bag and held it carefully so that she could look inside the envelope. It was empty. On the back of the envelope there were a few words: eggs, bread, milk, matches. Someone's shopping list. On the front was the name Morag Mackenzie but no address.

'You haven't had time to read Ronnie Campbell's police record,' said Grant, 'but the name Morag Mackenzie is in it. She's not one of his favourite people.'

Logan gave the bag and the envelope back to Helen.

'Helen, could you give this to the scientists,' she said. 'I want to know if there are any fingerprints on it. And I want to know if they can tell me anything about the handwriting.'

Logan turned to Grant. 'Well,' she said, 'it looks as if Ronnie Campbell may be dangerous. You'd better tell me what you know about him.'

Chapter 2 *A visit to Jimmy Brown*

'We were lucky to catch Campbell for Craig Sinclair's murder,' said Grant, as he and Logan walked down the hill towards her car.

'Did you work on the murder?' asked Logan.

'Yes, but before you ask, I didn't speak to Morag Mackenzie then and I don't know if that's her up there,' said Grant, pointing back up the hillside with his thumb. 'At first we didn't have any idea at all who'd killed Sinclair. Then someone rang the London Road police station, didn't leave a name, but said we should search Campbell's flat.'

'And what was there?' asked Logan.

'There was a gun in a metal box in his kitchen. It was the gun which had killed Sinclair. Campbell's fingerprints were all over the box.'

'What about the gun?'

'None. No fingerprints on the gun,' said Grant. 'He'd probably cleaned it. Anyway, they were still questioning him when Morag Mackenzie came into the police station. I wasn't there at the time. She said she'd seen Campbell and Sinclair drinking together and shouting at each other on the night that Sinclair died. The two of them had been in that pub at the end of Rose Street, the Abbotsford Arms.'

'What did Campbell have to say?' asked Logan.

'Well, he said the box was his but he'd never seen the gun. He also said he'd never been in the Abbotsford Arms in his life. He said he didn't know Sinclair very well at all so why would he kill him?'

'But you were sure you had the right person,' said Logan.

'Oh yes,' said Grant. 'Campbell had been in trouble quite a few times. He'd been to prison twice: once for stealing cars and once for fighting in a pub. He broke someone's arm.'

'That doesn't make him a murderer,' said Logan.

'True,' said Grant, 'but you wouldn't be surprised if he was.'

'What about Sinclair?' asked Logan.

'A small-time criminal, too. He'd never been to prison but that was just good luck. He got into fights; he sold stolen CDs, things like that.'

'Nice people,' said Logan.

At six o'clock, back at the London Road police station, Logan sent Grant to find out the latest news about Ronnie Campbell and the dark blue Audi. At last she had time to change out of her beach clothes into a dark blue trouser suit that she always kept in her office. She felt more comfortable at work if she wore smart clothes. She studied her face in the mirror. She had short brown hair and dark brown eyes, but she always thought her nose was rather too long. A journalist friend of hers, Tam MacDonald, said she was too pretty to be a police officer. She had been angry with him when he said this. She was intelligent and good at her job, and it was an important job. However, it was sometimes difficult being a woman police officer. Because she was good-looking, people did not always take her seriously. She worked hard to show those people they were wrong.

Logan got herself a cup of coffee. Then she opened Ronnie Campbell's record and looked at his photo. There was nothing interesting or unusual about him. He was thirty-five years old, 180 cm tall, with brown hair and brown eyes. The hair was short and straight, the eyes small and close together. He was described as slim and quite strong. As Logan looked at the photo, she began to ask herself questions. Why had Campbell escaped? Was that Morag Mackenzie's body in Holyrood Park? Had Morag seen Campbell in the Abbotsford Arms seven years ago? Had Campbell killed her? In fact, had he really killed Craig Sinclair? And where was he now? He wouldn't need new clothes because prisoners in Scotland wore their own clothes. But he would need money – where would he get it?

At that moment Grant returned.

'No news on Campbell or the Audi, I'm afraid,' he said. 'But I'm sure that was Morag Mackenzie's body on the hillside.'

'Why?' asked Logan.

'Some of the officers downstairs knew her and described her to me. She lived with a man called Jimmy Brown and he's no good at all. He's part of all sorts of criminal activities: robbery, stealing cars, everything.'

'We'll need him to look at the body so that we're sure it's her,' said Logan. 'And even though it seems Ronnie Campbell killed her, we'll also need to ask Mr Brown some questions. We need to know where he was this afternoon. As we know, women are most often murdered by their husband or boyfriend. Have you got an address for him?'

'Yes,' replied Grant. 'Springwell Place. Off Dalry Rd.'

'OK,' said Logan. 'Let's go.'

The flat which Jimmy Brown shared with Morag Mackenzie was on the second floor of an old building near Dalry Road. Grant parked the car in the street outside and followed Logan up the stairs. Their knock was answered by a young fair-haired man who badly needed a bath and a change of clothes. He was wearing a dirty red T-shirt, jeans which a long time ago had been white, and no shoes or socks. He was tall and looked down at Logan with an ugly smile on his face. He turned and looked at Grant and then back to Logan.

'Well,' he said, 'it's the pigs.'

Chapter 3 *The 'main man'*

People call the police a lot of different names: bobbies, coppers, the cops, and other worse things. The one thing all police officers really hate being called is 'pigs'. As soon as she heard the word, Logan felt Grant move beside her. She reached out her hand and put it on his arm.

'No,' she said softly. She looked at the man in front of her. 'Jimmy Brown?' she asked.

'Maybe,' he said. 'Who wants to know?'

'Jimmy, I'm Inspector Logan of the Edinburgh Police and this is Sergeant Grant.' She showed him her ID card then put it away in her bag.

'So?' said Jimmy, continuing to look down his nose at her.

'So we'd like to come in,' explained Grant, putting his face very close to the other man's face. Brown took a couple of steps back. Grant and Logan stepped quickly into the flat and Grant shut the door. Brown looked surprised.

'Problem?' asked Grant. His voice did not sound friendly. He did not look friendly.

Brown gave a weak smile and moved back against the wall.

Logan took a few more steps into the flat and looked around. She had been in some terrible flats in the past but she had never seen anywhere quite like this. The furniture was old and had cigarette burns all over it. The walls were a dark colour; probably once a kind of brown but it was difficult to tell. Coffee cups and cigarette packets lay everywhere. Empty pizza boxes lay on the table; that day's evening paper was open on a chair; a half-eaten piece of pizza lay on the floor by an empty beer can on its side. There was a smell of unwashed clothes and unwashed people.

She turned to Jimmy Brown.

'Do you know where Morag is, Jimmy?'

Brown moved away from Grant and walked round the room picking up empty cigarette packets and shaking them.

'No,' he said.

'What were you doing this afternoon?'

'Nothing.'

'Come on, Jimmy, let's have some answers,' said Logan, impatiently.

Grant looked round the room. There was a door to his left. He reached out to open it.

'Don't go in there,' said Brown, moving towards Grant.

Grant looked once at Brown and opened the door.

'Well, well, well,' said Grant, sounding very pleased with himself, as he looked through the door he had just opened. 'What have we got here?'

Logan took a step forward to see what Grant had found. There was a bed in one corner of the room, but all along the opposite wall were boxes of videos, televisions and CD players all on top of each other. Grant walked into the room and opened some of the boxes, checking what was inside.

Brown sat down on the floor in the living room, looking unhappily at the wall on the other side of the room.

'Am I right in thinking that these are all stolen?' asked Logan.

Brown nodded but did not speak.

'It's not your lucky day, is it?' continued Logan. 'You're in big trouble now, Jimmy. And it'll be much worse if we don't get some answers. So where's Morag?'

'I really don't know,' said Brown. 'She went out about midday.'

'Where? Was she working?'

'No, she doesn't work much,' said Brown. 'Not a real job, anyway. Not a nine to five kind of job.'

'Where does she get money?' asked Logan, as Grant came back into the living room.

'I really don't know,' said Brown very quickly. 'Some man. She calls him her "main man". She gets money from him sometimes.'

'You're joking,' said Grant. 'You expect us to believe that some man just gives Morag money. Why? What does she do?'

'It's true. Really. It's true. I don't know what she does for him.'

'You don't know who this "main man" is, then?' asked Logan.

'No,' said Brown.

'No idea?' asked Grant, looking hard at Brown.

'I think he's someone important,' said Brown quickly, 'but she's never told me. She always says there are some things it's better not to know.'

'So you don't know what she did for him?'

'No,' said Brown.

'Was she going to see him today?' asked Logan.

'Probably,' said Brown. 'She made a phone call just before she went out. It sounded as if she was talking to him. In fact, it sounded as if she wanted to see him. Why are you asking all these questions about Morag anyway? What's she done?'

Logan stopped speaking. She looked out of the window and thought about the main man. How important was he? Grant continued the questioning.

'What about you, Jimmy?' he asked. 'Where have you been all day?'

'Here,' said Brown. 'I've been here. I haven't been out all day.'

'Is there anyone who's seen you or been with you?' Grant asked.

'No,' said Brown.

'No visitors?'

'No.'

Brown got up off the floor and started looking a little braver than before.

'Now, come on, you two. I've answered your questions,' he said. 'What's all this about? What's Morag been doing?'

Logan looked at Grant. Grant sat down on the arm of the cleanest chair.

'Jimmy,' he said, 'you'd better sit down. I'm afraid I've got some bad news for you.'

* * *

They drove from Jimmy Brown's flat to the London Road police station. Grant and Logan sat in the front of the car, Brown in the back. He had cried when Grant told him about Morag. When he had stopped crying, they told him he would have to come to the police station. He would have to look at the body so that they could be sure it was Morag. He would also have to talk to officers from the Robbery Unit about what was in his bedroom. Logan didn't tell him that she would have some more questions for him later.

As Grant drove, Logan thought about the people who had come into her life today: Ronnie Campbell, murderer; Jimmy Brown, robber; Morag Mackenzie, dead at the age of . . . How old was she? Twenty-six? Twenty-seven? Certainly not much older.

When they arrived at the police station, it was seven thirty. Logan asked a young sergeant to take Brown to look at the body. As soon as they had left, she turned to Grant.

'He wasn't telling the truth about this afternoon,' she said.

'Wasn't he?' asked Grant.

'No,' replied Logan. 'He had this evening's paper in the flat. The evening paper comes out at about two o'clock. So either he went out to buy it or a visitor brought it in.'

'You didn't question him about it,' said Grant.

'No. I thought I'd leave it till later,' said Logan. 'He might talk more easily here.'

Grant smiled and then said, 'He's left-handed.'

'Yes, I saw,' said Logan. 'And tall.'

'And he's not a very nice person.'

'No,' said Logan. 'But that doesn't make him a murderer.'

'True,' said Grant. 'But you wouldn't . . . '

'. . . be surprised if he was,' finished Logan, smiling. 'And what about the main man?' she asked.

'It's an interesting choice of words, isn't it?' said Grant.

'Yes,' said Logan. 'It is unusual. But I've heard it before.'

'Someone who thinks they're important,' said Grant, more to himself than to Logan.

'Right,' said Logan, putting a hand on Grant's shoulder. 'When Jimmy's had a look at the body, lock him up and get someone from the Robbery Unit to go and talk to him about all those stolen things. They'll also need to go round to his flat and pick everything up. Then come and find me in my office.'

'Right,' said Grant.

* * *

Logan was reading through Ronnie Campbell's police record and making notes in a small black notebook when Grant returned. As he came through the door, she looked at her watch. It was eight fifteen but it was still very light outside.

'The body is Morag Mackenzie's,' Grant told Logan.

'Yes, someone rang to tell me,' she replied. 'Any news on the envelope or the knife?'

'The scientists will call us as soon as possible about the envelope. The search has finished and they haven't found a knife.'

'What about St Margaret's Loch? Maybe the killer threw the knife in the water,' said Logan. St Margaret's Loch was a small man-made lake in Holyrood Park. 'Get some divers to check that in the morning.'

'Right, madam,' said Grant.

'Do we have any idea where Campbell might go?' she asked.

'Not really,' said Grant. 'I spoke to the prison. He had one visitor in the last twelve months: his lawyer.'

'Of course, at this time of year it's warm enough to sleep outside,' Logan said. She went on: 'I've also been thinking about how he'll get money.'

'He'll probably steal it,' said Grant.

Logan said nothing for a few moments. Then she spoke: 'Campbell was sent to prison for fifteen years.'

'That's right,' said Grant.

'He's still got quite a long time left,' said Logan.

'Yes,' agreed Grant. 'And because he's in trouble again now, he won't get out early. He'll be in there for eight more years.'

'There's something strange about this murder,' said Logan. 'I think if we want to find out who murdered Morag Mackenzie we'll need to look into Craig Sinclair's murder again.'

Grant looked at her but said nothing. He had only worked with Inspector Logan for three years, but he knew that she was often right.

Logan looked through a few pages of her notebook.

'Craig Sinclair had a sister,' she said. 'Jean Drummond, married. There's an address for her in the New Town, St Stephen Street. Let's see if she still lives there. Go and organise the divers for tomorrow and I'll meet you in the car park in ten minutes.'

'What about Jimmy Brown?' asked Grant.

'Let the Robbery Unit talk to him tonight,' said Logan.

'We'll talk to him tomorrow. I'm more interested in finding out about Sinclair's murder at the moment.'

The Old Town of Edinburgh is a fairly small area around the Castle and the Palace of Holyroodhouse. St Stephen Street is in the New Town, not far from Princes Street. And although this part of the city is already more than two hundred years old, it is still called the New Town.

As they drove through the streets of Edinburgh at eight thirty on this warm June evening, Logan looked at the busy streets and the stone houses. She thought to herself, as she often did, that Edinburgh must be one of the most beautiful cities in the world. She had been to London once but she hadn't liked it. London was too big, too noisy, too dirty. Edinburgh was just right.

As they turned into St Stephen Street and parked, the car phone rang. Grant picked it up. He listened for a minute, then said goodbye and put the phone down.

'They've found the Audi,' he said. 'In a car park near the Haymarket Station.'

'That's near Dalry Road,' said Logan, 'where Morag Mackenzie was living.'

'Yes. They're searching the area but Campbell could be anywhere by now. He won't go back to the car. That would be completely stupid.'

'True,' said Logan. 'OK. Let's go and see what Sinclair's sister has to say.'

Chapter 4 *Bags of money*

St Stephen Street is a narrow street with tall buildings on each side. Almost all the buildings are now flats; a couple are pubs and there are a few shops. Grant and Logan walked up the steps to the front door of one of the buildings and studied the names on the wall next to the door.

'Drummond. First floor.' Grant pointed to the name.

Logan and Grant walked up the stairs. Grant knocked at a door and it was opened by a woman in her early thirties.

'Yes?' said the woman.

'Mrs Jean Drummond?' asked Logan.

'Yes.'

'I'm Inspector Logan, Edinburgh Police,' said Logan. 'I'm sorry it's so late. Could I have a few words with you, please?'

'Of course,' said Jean Drummond. 'Come in.'

Jean Drummond had shoulder-length blonde hair, blue eyes and a warm smile. She was wearing jeans and a shirt that was too big and almost came down to her knees.

'Sorry about all this,' she said, pointing to tables and chairs on top of each other and several boxes of books on the floor. 'I'm painting the living room. I was going to do it when we came here eight years ago and I've finally started. Come into the kitchen and sit down. Would you like a cup of tea?'

'Thank you,' said Logan. 'That would be nice.'

Grant and Logan sat down on wooden chairs by the kitchen table while Jean Drummond made some tea. The kitchen was clean and welcoming. Yellow walls, yellow curtains. It was light and airy. It felt comfortable to sit in. Logan couldn't think of anywhere more different from Jimmy Brown's flat.

'I'm afraid we've come to ask you some questions about your brother, Craig, and his death,' said Logan. 'I'm sorry to come round and ask about the past, but it might be important.'

Jean Drummond put some cups and a teapot on the table and looked at Logan. She was no longer smiling but her eyes still seemed soft and warm.

'Inspector, don't worry about the past. I don't. I was very sad when Craig was killed but it was no great surprise. He was often in trouble. Even when he was a boy he was in trouble at school. By the time he was fourteen, the police were always coming round to our house to speak to him. I was sad when he died. Very sad. I mean, he was my brother and I loved him. But . . .'

She stopped speaking and passed tea to Logan and then to Grant.

'Mrs Drummond,' said Logan, 'I don't know if you've heard the news today, but Ronnie Campbell, the man who was in prison for the murder of your brother, has escaped.'

Jean Drummond put down her cup. Logan and Grant could almost see the different thoughts going through her head.

'And the girl who said she saw Campbell with your brother on the night he died was murdered today.'

Jean Drummond's hand flew up to her mouth and she made a strange low sound. Logan reached out and put her hand softly on the woman's arm.

'Don't worry,' Logan said. 'Campbell won't be interested in you.'

Jean Drummond's eyes were wide open. She looked very afraid. 'But he might be,' she said. Her voice sounded very worried. 'Campbell always said that he didn't really know Craig at all, but I always thought they were friends. I saw them together five or six times at least. I thought they were probably working together, stealing and so on. That's what I told the police. And I'm sure Campbell won't have forgotten that.'

Logan and Grant looked at each other. Then Logan turned to Jean Drummond. 'I really don't think you're in any danger,' she said, 'but of course we can't take any chances. We could ask for a policewoman to stay with you until we find Campbell.'

Jean Drummond sat quietly for a moment, thinking.

'Yes, I think I would like that,' she said finally. 'My husband is away on business at the moment and I don't want to be in the flat alone.'

Logan nodded at Grant, who went out of the room to phone for a policewoman.

Logan spoke to Jean Drummond again. 'You said your brother was often in trouble with the police?'

'Yes. I always knew Craig was a criminal,' she said. 'I mean, he always had money and he never had a job. For a long time I thought he was just a small criminal. You know, buying and selling things that were stolen. Perhaps stealing things himself sometimes as well. I used to think that he wasn't a serious criminal and that one day he'd grow up and get a job.'

Grant came quietly back into the room and sat down. Logan said nothing, waiting to see if Jean Drummond wanted to say more.

'I haven't thought about Craig for a long time,' said Jean, standing up and looking out of the window down to the street below. 'I always thought he would leave his life of crime. But one evening he came round to see me. He'd had too much to drink and he was full of talk about money. I saw then that he had decided how he would live his life. I saw then that he would always be a criminal.'

Again Logan said nothing. Sometimes it was better to let people follow their thoughts.

Jean Drummond turned back from the window with a little smile on her face. 'I'd almost forgotten about that evening. I remember Craig said something strange. He said something like "I'm going to get bags of money." I thought he meant he was going to get lots of money. I thought he was telling me that he was going to become very rich, so I said something like "That'll be nice to have bags of money." But he said, "No. No. I'm going to get bags of money. He thinks he's Mr Big around here . . . " I asked him who he was talking about, but he just repeated "bags of money". I don't know what he meant. Anyway, he'd had far too much to drink so it probably didn't mean anything.'

Jean Drummond did not see Grant look across at Logan, but Logan did. Grant had got something. It was something that the woman had said. Logan couldn't think what it was and she would have to wait to find out.

Jean Drummond was smiling to herself, remembering her brother.

'I haven't thought about that for ages,' she said, as she sat down on one of the kitchen chairs. 'I'm sorry. You must think I can't stop talking. It's just that I haven't talked about Craig for ages.'

'No. You don't have to be sorry,' said Logan. 'Thank you for seeing us. You've been very helpful.'

After telling Jean Drummond that a policewoman would arrive in about half an hour, Logan and Grant said goodbye and left the flat. As they walked down the stairs, Logan looked at Grant.

'OK,' she said. 'What did Jean Drummond say that was so interesting?'

'Well,' said Grant. 'Craig Sinclair had drunk far too much. What if he didn't say he was going to get "bags of money"? What if he actually said he was going to get "Bags's money"?'

'And who,' asked Logan, 'is Bags?'

Grant gave her a big smile.

Chapter 5 *Questions for Robert Baxter*

'Bags,' said Grant as he opened the car door and got in, 'is Robert Baxter.'

'You mean the Robert Baxter who owns the big sports centre out on the Corstorphine Road?' asked Logan.

'That's him. And, of course, the Robert Baxter that the Serious Crimes Unit have been trying to catch for such a long time.'

'How is it that you know he's called Bags and I don't?' said Logan, smiling. When she and Grant had started working together three years ago, Logan had quickly realised that Grant was a very good policeman. He had ways of getting information that other people couldn't find out, and he forgot very little.

'I'd be surprised if you did know he's called Bags,' said Grant. 'Only people who grew up in Edinburgh would know.'

Logan was from Penicuik, a town about fifteen kilometres south of Edinburgh.

'Baxter grew up in a poor part of town,' continued Grant. 'He was a wild kid, but he only got caught by the police once.'

'What for?' asked Logan, as she knew Grant wanted her to.

'For stealing an old lady's handbag. He ran past her in the street and took it. Unluckily for him, he ran straight into the arms of a policeman. After that, his friends called him 'Bags' Baxter for a while.'

'But not now?' asked Logan.

'No, he's too rich and important now,' said Grant. 'And, of course, people are afraid of him.'

'Yes,' said Logan, 'they certainly are.'

For the rest of the journey back to the London Road police station, neither Grant nor Logan spoke. Logan was deep in thought about Robert Baxter.

The Serious Crimes Unit had wanted to catch Baxter for a long time but he'd been too clever. Baxter was the man behind a lot of the crime in Edinburgh. He planned it, organised it and made a lot of money from it. He also owned businesses that were not criminal and made a lot of money from those too. Baxter was a hard man. He expected the people who worked for him to do what they were told without question. People who did not follow his orders found out how hard he was. It was said that he had killed more than one person. However, the police had never found anything and it was difficult for them to get information about Baxter because people were too afraid to talk.

When Logan and Grant arrived back at the London Road police station, it was nearly ten o'clock. Logan spoke: 'We'll need to talk to Mr Baxter tomorrow, Grant. Find out where he's going to be at nine thirty in the morning and let me know before you go home.'

'Right, madam,' said Grant.

Logan went up to her office. On her desk were two notes from the scientists. The first note said that there were three fingerprints on the envelope. Two of them were Morag

Mackenzies's; one was not. That fingerprint might be useful if they could find out whose it was. There was no information about the handwriting on the front of the envelope. The writing on the back was Morag's. The second note said that the scientists were looking at the blue Audi and they would let Logan know what they found out the next day.

Logan turned her chair away from her desk and sat looking out of the window. She thought about the two people who were dead: Craig Sinclair, killed seven years ago, and Morag Mackenzie, killed not much more than seven hours ago. Were they killed by different people or was it perhaps the same person? Why had Ronnie Campbell escaped? Had he killed Morag because she had helped to put him in prison? Would he kill again? Or was there another reason for his escape? What about Jimmy Brown? Was he just a robber? Or was he a murderer too? And now there was Robert Baxter. What was his part in this story? Was he left-handed or right-handed? She would find out in the morning.

* * *

At nine thirty the next morning Logan and Grant were standing beside an indoor tennis court at the Robert Baxter Sports Centre watching two men play tennis. The taller of the two, fair-haired and in his late thirties, threw a ball in the air and hit it hard with the racket in his right hand. Logan knew from pictures she had seen in the papers that this was Robert Baxter. The other man missed the ball completely.

'Game, set and match,' said Baxter. 'Six love, six two.'

The men shook hands. 'Thanks for the game,' said Baxter.

As Baxter came off the court, Logan and Grant walked up to him.

'Mr Baxter, I'm Inspector Logan of the Edinburgh Police and this is Sergeant Grant.' Logan showed him her ID card. 'I was hoping we could talk to you for a few minutes.'

'Of course, Inspector,' said Baxter. 'I'm always happy to help the police.' His voice was friendly but Logan looked into his eyes. They were grey and hard.

'If it's all right with you, Inspector,' said Baxter, 'I'd like to have a quick shower first and then we could talk in my office.'

'OK,' agreed Logan.

'There are some seats by the front entrance,' said Baxter. 'If you wait there, I'll be very quick.'

Ten minutes later, Baxter led Logan and Grant through the sports centre towards his office. Logan watched Baxter walking easily in front of her. His suit looked Italian and Logan thought it must have cost at least £1500. Baxter was also wearing a dark blue shirt with a light blue tie. There was a large gold ring on the little finger of his left hand. And his shoes, which looked Italian too, probably cost as much as the suit. Here was a man who liked spending his money on clothes.

They arrived at Baxter's office and he held the door open for Logan and Grant to walk in. It was a large airy room with expensive-looking furniture.

'Coffee?' asked Baxter, nodding at the coffee machine on a small table at the side of the room.

'No, thank you,' said Logan. 'We'll try to take as little of your time as possible. We know you're a busy man.'

Baxter got a cup of coffee for himself and sat down opposite Logan and Grant.

'What can I do for you, Inspector?' he asked. He took a cigarette from a wooden box on his desk and lit it with a gold lighter.

'Just a couple of things, really,' said Logan. 'A young woman was murdered yesterday in Holyrood Park.'

'Yes, I read about it in the paper this morning,' said Baxter. 'A terrible business.'

'Her name was Morag Mackenzie. Have you ever met her or spoken to her?'

Baxter thought for a moment or two.

'Morag Mackenzie,' he said slowly. 'No, I don't think I know that name. Of course, she might have used the sports centre here. I could get someone to find out, if you like. I mean, I know some of the people who come here but not all of them. There are far too many.'

'That's all right,' said Logan. 'I don't think she was a very sporty type of person.' She gave a little smile and then continued. 'The other question is about the past. Did you ever know a man called Craig Sinclair? Did he work for you or were you friends with him?'

Baxter looked as if he was thinking hard. His hand came up to his chin. 'Craig Sinclair. No, I don't think so. I don't think I know that name at all. Again, I could get someone to find out if he was working here but . . .' Baxter did not finish the sentence.

'Well, that's it,' said Logan, standing up.

'I'm sorry I couldn't be more help, Inspector,' said Baxter, also standing up. 'I hope you find the person you're looking for.'

'I hope so too,' said Logan. She looked round at Baxter's office. 'You've done very well for yourself, Mr Baxter. I understand you come from one of the poorer parts of Edinburgh, and yet now you're an important businessman with a number of fine companies.'

'I've worked hard,' said Baxter, smiling a little. 'If I do something, I like to do it well. Now, if you'll excuse me,' he continued, picking up the phone, 'I have an important call to make.'

As Logan and Grant left the room, they could hear Baxter speaking.

'What do you mean he's not there?' he said. 'Find out where he is. Tell him the main man wants to speak to him.'

Outside the sports centre, Logan and Grant sat in the car. Across the car park Logan could see a dark green Mercedes. The car number was RB 1.

'So,' said Logan, 'do you think Baxter is Morag Mackenzie's main man?'

'That's just the question I was asking myself,' said Grant. 'But even if he is, that doesn't mean he killed her. Anyway, he's right-handed.'

Logan put on her seat belt and started the car. 'What did you think of him?' she asked.

'I think his clothes probably cost as much money as I earn in a month,' said Grant.

'I didn't know you were so interested in fashion,' said Logan, and they both laughed. Grant always wore a blue jacket and grey trousers. Somehow, even when he wore a new jacket or new trousers, they always looked old.

'There was something else strange though,' she said.

'What was that?' asked Grant.

'He didn't seem at all surprised by the questions.'

'How do you mean?' asked Grant.

'Well, he didn't want to know why we were asking him about these two people,' replied Logan. 'I mean, if someone started asking you questions about two people you'd never heard of, wouldn't you want to know why?'

'I see what you mean,' said Grant. 'Yes, that is interesting. I hadn't thought of that.'

As Logan turned the car out of the sports centre on to Corstorphine Road, the car phone rang. Grant answered it.

He listened for a moment then said, 'Hold on, please.' He turned to Logan.

'I think you might want to take this call. It's your journalist friend, Tam MacDonald. He says he knows where Ronnie Campbell is.'

Chapter 6 *Catching Ronnie Campbell*

Logan stopped the car at the side of the road. She and Grant quickly got out and changed places so that he could drive. As she got back into the car, she picked up the phone.

'Tam,' she said, 'are you doing my job for me again?'

There was a laugh at the other end of the phone.

'Jenny, my dear,' Tam's voice came down the phone, 'I could never do it as well as you do.'

Logan laughed too.

'Seriously,' said Tam, 'I heard that you were leading the search for Ronnie Campbell. Well, I'm looking at him right now.'

'Where are you?' asked Logan.

'Well, he's sitting on the ground outside Jenner's department store in Princes Street holding out his hat for people to put money in,' said Tam, 'and I'm on the other side of the road looking like a tourist.'

Logan looked at Grant. 'Jenner's, Princes Street. Quick,' she said.

Grant turned on the blue light, put it out on the roof of the car and pulled into the traffic.

'You could never look like a tourist, Tam,' said Logan into the phone.

Tam laughed. Like quite a few Scots, he had red hair.

Logan spoke into the phone again, 'Are you sure it's Campbell?'

'I am now,' said Tam. 'At first I thought he was just another beggar who lives on the street and asks people for money.'

'How clever of him!' said Logan.

'What do you mean?' asked Tam.

'Well, his photo is in the papers and on the television and everyone's looking for him,' said Logan.

'So?' said Tam.

'So, nobody looks at street people,' she explained. 'It's the best place to hide. He's right in front of us, but in a place we'd never think to look. It explains how he's getting money, too.'

'Very clever,' agreed Tam.

'You're sure it's him, aren't you?' Logan asked suddenly.

'Oh yes,' said Tam, 'I wrote one or two pieces about the Sinclair murder so I know what Campbell looks like.'

'Keep your eye on him.'

'Sure,' said Tam. 'But listen, I followed him to Jenner's from Holyrood Park.'

'Holyrood Park?' repeated Logan. 'What was he doing there?'

'I've no idea. I went out there to have a look at where Morag Mackenzie was murdered. As I was leaving, I saw Campbell. So I left my car in the park and followed him on foot up here. I waited until he stopped somewhere before I rang you.'

'We'll be there in a few minutes,' said Logan, 'so wait for us.'

'Don't worry,' said Tam, 'I'll be waiting around for my dinner invitation after giving you information like this.'

Logan laughed.

'I'll see you in a few minutes,' she said, and turned her phone off. It was unusual for a police officer and a journalist to be close friends but she and Tam were.

The road was fairly clear as they reached the Haymarket, and two minutes later they were at the west end of Princes Street. Grant turned off the light and brought it inside the car again. They drove slowly along the street with the rest of the traffic. Jenner's was at the far end of Princes Street on their left. As Logan looked along the street in front of her, she could see a man sitting in front of the department store. There was a hat on the ground next to him.

'I'll get out here,' she said, getting out quickly and shutting the door as Grant stopped the car.

Grant drove on again and stopped just past the front door of the store. He got out and walked back quickly.

Logan and Grant walked towards Ronnie Campbell at the same time. As they got near, he looked up and suddenly realised they were police officers. He moved faster than seemed possible. In seconds he was on his feet and running across the road. Cars had to stop suddenly and there was a loud noise of screaming metal and breaking glass, as other cars hit those that had stopped.

'Police! Stop!' shouted Grant, running across the road after Campbell. Logan followed, pulling her phone out of her pocket to call for help. As Campbell reached the other side of the road, he turned right, running fast along the side of the road looking for a way into the Princes Street Gardens. Suddenly, a short red-haired person jumped out of the crowd and threw his arms round Campbell's legs. It was Tam MacDonald. MacDonald and Campbell fell to the ground, with Campbell fighting to get away. Seconds later Grant arrived. He pulled one of Campbell's arms round behind his back and pushed it up between his shoulders. Campbell stopped fighting and lay there on the ground. Then Logan arrived, pulled her police ID card out of her pocket and showed it to Campbell.

'Ronnie Campbell,' she said, 'you're wanted for escaping from a prison van near Dundee yesterday morning, for stealing a car, and we've got a lot of other questions we want to ask you too. So get on your feet and we're all going down to the London Road police station.'

She turned to Tam MacDonald, who was getting to his feet and brushing down his clothes with his hands. He was wearing jeans, a dark green T-shirt and a brown jacket.

'Hi, Jenny,' he said to Logan.

'Well done, Tam!' she said. 'I didn't know you were good at rugby.'

'Actually, I played for the first team at school,' said Tam with a big smile.

Chapter 7 *A very good reason to kill*

Back at the London Road police station, Logan and Grant sat opposite Campbell in a windowless room. The clock on the wall showed eleven thirty. A cassette recorder on the table recorded their conversation. Ronnie sat forward in his chair, his arms on the table, his head in his hands. He was wearing a white T-shirt, jeans and trainers. A blue jacket was on the back of his chair. A paper cup of water was on the table in front of him. Since they had brought him into the room he had said nothing.

Logan waited until Campbell looked up at her. 'Why did you escape, Ronnie?' she asked.

Campbell looked her straight in the eye. 'Because I wanted to get out,' he replied.

'Don't play games with us,' said Grant crossly. 'You know what the inspector means.'

Campbell looked at Grant and said nothing.

Logan spoke again. 'Ronnie, you know that first, almost no-one escapes. Second, if you do escape, you are almost certainly caught. Third, the only way to stay free is to have friends outside to give you money and get you out of the country. And you don't have any friends outside, do you?'

Campbell said nothing. Logan and Grant said nothing. The room stayed quiet.

After a few minutes Logan said, 'Do you remember the girl who said she saw you and Sinclair in the Abbotsford Arms?'

Campbell looked up again. This time his eyes looked hard. He still said nothing.

'Do you remember her name?' asked Logan.

Campbell said nothing. Logan looked at Grant.

'Come on, Ronnie,' said Grant. 'I've told you – stop the games. You remember Morag Mackenzie. You won't forget her name quickly, will you? Well, she was killed yesterday, soon after you escaped. In fact probably about the time you got to Edinburgh. Someone cut her throat.'

There was a strange look on Ronnie's face: he looked surprised and afraid.

Grant continued: 'The inspector asked why you escaped. My answer is that you've spent seven years in prison because of Morag Mackenzie and you've still got time left to spend there. Morag Mackenzie gave the police important information that meant you were caught and sent to prison. I think you escaped so you could find Morag and murder her . . .'

Campbell jumped up out of his chair.

'Stop it!' he shouted. 'I didn't kill Morag Mackenzie and I didn't kill Craig Sinclair. I didn't even know Morag Mackenzie was dead.'

'But you did know where she lived, didn't you?' said Logan. She wasn't at all sure that he did know but it seemed possible since the blue Audi was found near her flat.

'Yes, I did,' Campbell said. 'I know someone who knows her.'

'So what happened when you went to see her?' said Logan. Again she didn't know that he had been to see Morag but it seemed possible; probable even.

'I didn't see her,' said Campbell.

'You were seen,' said Grant, following Logan's thoughts and letting Campbell think they knew more than they actually did. 'We found the car near her flat and you were seen going there.'

'I went there,' said Campbell, 'but she wasn't in. There was no-one there.'

'So where was Jimmy Brown?' Logan thought to herself. Then she remembered the evening paper in Morag's flat and realised that Brown must have gone out at some point.

'So what did you do then?' she asked.

'Well, I just walked the streets for a time.'

'Weren't you worried that someone might realise who you were from your picture in the papers or on the television?' asked Logan.

Campbell looked at Logan. 'Nobody looks at people who live on the street,' he said.

Logan nodded slowly and then looked at Grant.

'Where did you spend the night?' Grant asked Campbell.

'Holyrood Park.'

'Had you been there before?' asked Grant.

'What do you mean "before"?' said Campbell.

'Before yesterday evening,' explained Grant.

'No,' said Campbell. 'I got there about ten or eleven in the evening. It was already dark. I slept up on the hillside about halfway up Arthur's Seat.'

It seemed to Logan that Campbell was beginning to talk more freely. Perhaps he might give her the information she had wanted earlier.

'So why did you want to see Morag Mackenzie?' she asked.

Campbell was quiet for a few moments, putting his thoughts together and deciding if he should answer at all.

'You wouldn't understand,' he said at last.

'Try me,' said Logan.

'I was beginning to go mad in prison. It's a terrible place. More terrible than you can possibly know. Seven years is a long time. I didn't know how long I could last. And I was in there for something I didn't do.'

Campbell stopped and looked at Logan and Grant, waiting for them to say they did not believe him. They stayed quiet, knowing that if they spoke, Campbell would say nothing more.

'For a time I thought there would be some new information about Sinclair's murder,' continued Campbell. 'I hoped the police would find out who really did it. But my lawyer came to see me some time ago and said that there was no chance of that happening.'

He stopped for a moment and drank some water. 'I had no hope. No hope of getting out. No hope of people believing that I didn't kill Sinclair. No hope. And then there was a chance to escape so I took it. I didn't think about it. I just took the chance when it came.'

'And Morag?' asked Logan quietly.

'She hadn't told the truth,' said Campbell, 'and I wanted to know why. I wanted to find out why she had said she'd seen us together the night Sinclair was murdered. I didn't even know her. Perhaps someone had paid her to say it. But if so, who? And why? I wanted to find out.'

'So, what were your plans for today?' asked Logan.

'I was hoping to get some more money outside Jenner's this morning and then go and see if Morag was back at her place this afternoon.'

Logan and Grant left a police officer with Campbell and went up to Logan's office for some coffee.

'So, what do you think?' asked Logan.

'Well, he didn't have a knife, or blood all over his clothes,' said Grant.

'But he does have a very good reason for wanting to kill her,' Logan said.

'Seven years in prison,' said Grant.

Logan picked up a message from her desk and read it.

'The search of Morag and Jimmy's flat,' she said. 'The scientists have taken away some knives for a closer look, but no clothes with blood on them.'

She picked up another note from her desk.

'Campbell's fingerprints are on the inside of the blue Audi, but there's nothing else of interest there. They're also checking the fingerprints on the envelope with our records. So far they aren't Campbell's or Jimmy Brown's.'

She looked at her watch.

'I think we should go and talk to Jimmy Brown now,' she said. 'I want to know how that newspaper got into his flat and if he really knew who Morag's main man was.'

Chapter 8 *The mystery car*

'Sorry you've had to wait so long,' said Logan sweetly, as she and Grant came into the room where Jimmy Brown was sitting. It was just after one o'clock. 'We've been rather busy,' she added.

Brown just looked at her angrily.

'Been having an interesting conversation with the Robbery Unit?' asked Grant, sitting down on one of the chairs opposite Brown.

'I've been up half the night answering questions,' said Brown. 'Why don't you go away and leave me alone? I know I'm in trouble for the stolen things in the flat. But I had nothing to do with Morag's murder. Just go away and leave me alone.'

Logan sat on the other chair opposite Brown and looked at him. 'Jimmy, I just want to find the person who killed Morag,' said Logan. 'Now, where were you yesterday?'

'At home,' said Brown. 'I told you.'

'I know that's what you told us,' said Logan, 'but that wasn't the truth, was it?' As she said this, she looked Brown straight in the eye. Jimmy looked back for a few seconds but then looked away and started to bite his lip.

'I followed Morag,' he said softly.

No-one spoke.

'I didn't kill her.' Brown spoke again. 'Really I didn't.'

'Why didn't you tell us this before?' asked Logan.

'I know what the police are like. Just because I've been in

trouble before, you think you can get me for anything now. It doesn't matter what I tell you. You're all the same. So why should I tell you anything? And now, because I didn't tell you the truth, you're going to think that I killed Morag.' Brown was beginning to get angry again.

'Jimmy,' said Logan patiently, 'You're a criminal and I don't like you. But you don't have to be afraid of me if you didn't murder Morag.'

Jimmy gave Logan a strange look. Police officers didn't often say things like that, not to people like him anyway.

'So why did you decide to follow Morag?' asked Logan.

Brown looked down at the table as if deciding if he should tell the truth or not. Finally, he looked at Grant and then at Logan. 'I wanted to find out who the main man was.'

'Why?' asked Logan. 'Why now? Why not before?'

'Well, Morag and I'd only known each other six months. We only got the flat together a couple of months ago. I didn't want to put my nose into her business too early. So I waited. Until now. I thought it was time to find out who the main man was.'

'And did you find out?' asked Grant.

'No,' said Brown.

'Let's go back to before Morag went out,' said Logan. 'When we spoke to you at the flat, you said that Morag made a phone call.'

'That's right,' said Brown.

'You thought she wanted to meet her main man.'

'Yes,' said Brown.

'Did she usually ring him or did he ring her?' asked Logan.

Brown gave Logan another strange look. 'Yes, yesterday was unusual. He usually rang her. In fact, I don't think I can ever remember her calling him except for yesterday.'

'So why do you think she called him yesterday?' asked Logan.

'I don't know,' said Brown, thinking hard.

'What were you doing before she called him?' asked Logan.

'Watching TV. Then suddenly she jumped up and made the phone call. I just thought she'd forgotten something.'

'What time did this happen?' asked Logan.

'I don't know. Midday maybe. Yes, it must have been around that time because we were watching the midday news.'

'OK,' said Logan. 'Now what time did you say Morag went out?'

'Soon after that,' replied Brown.

Logan looked at Grant and he started to ask the questions. 'Where did she go?' he said.

'She walked down Dalry Road towards the Haymarket,' said Brown. 'And then this car stopped beside her. She got in the car. And that was it. The car drove away.'

Logan sat back in her chair, thinking. Campbell's escape would have been on the midday news. Morag must have seen that and phoned her main man. She started listening to Grant and Brown again.

'What kind of car?' asked Grant.

'Don't know,' said Brown.

'Big, small?' asked Grant.

'Big,' said Brown, 'and a dark colour. Blue or green or something.'

Grant and Logan looked at each other.

'Which?' asked Logan. 'Blue or green?'

'I don't remember.'

'Did you see the car number?' Logan asked.

'Oh come on, Inspector,' said Brown. 'It was just a car.'

'What was the person in the car like?' continued Grant.

'I don't know. This all happened about fifty metres away. I couldn't see very much.'

'Think back,' said Logan. 'Remember what happened. Did you see anything else?'

'No. Nothing.'

'Which way did they drive away?' asked Grant.

'They drove up towards the Haymarket,' said Brown.

'And what did you do?' asked Grant.

'I went back home,' said Brown.

'But first you bought a newspaper,' said Logan.

'How do you know that?' asked Brown.

'I'm a detective,' said Logan, and smiled.

'Come on, Jimmy,' Grant said. 'What do you think Morag did for the main man? You must have an idea.'

'She went to parties and looked after some of the people he did business with, if you know what I mean. Talked to people and made them feel welcome.'

'And she slept with them?' asked Grant.

'Yes, and that,' said Brown quietly. 'That's another reason we didn't talk about it too much.'

'Did Morag ever talk about someone called Robert Baxter?' asked Logan.

Brown's eyes suddenly opened wide in surprise. 'Robert Baxter! Is he the main man?' he asked.

'You know him?' asked Logan.

‘Everyone knows Robert Baxter,’ said Brown. ‘I mean, I don’t know him really and I don’t want to know him. But I know who he is.’

‘Is it possible that he was the main man?’ asked Logan.

Brown’s shoulders went up and then down. ‘It’s possible,’ he said. ‘But Morag never talked about him.’

‘Did she talk much about the past?’ Logan asked.

‘Not really,’ Brown said.

‘Did she ever talk about Craig Sinclair?’

‘Craig Sinclair? That little rat! No, she didn’t talk about him.’ Brown was angry again. His eyes had lit up. ‘But I remember him. He once sold me a couple of boxes full of CDs and then the next day the police came round to my place and found them. He promised me he hadn’t told the police where to find them. I didn’t know if I believed him or not. I got into big trouble for that. The little rat!’

‘Of course, he was murdered as well,’ said Logan quietly.

Logan watched Brown’s face as he suddenly realised talking about Craig Sinclair like that might be a mistake.

‘Hey! Come on,’ he said. ‘I know he was murdered. I didn’t like him but that doesn’t mean I killed him.’

* * *

Later, Logan and Grant were sitting in Logan’s office drinking coffee. They had taken Brown through his story again, but he hadn’t added anything or changed any of it.

‘Should we believe Jimmy Brown?’ asked Grant.

‘I don’t know,’ said Logan, shaking her head. ‘It’s strange that he knew Sinclair as well. We’ll need to check what Brown was doing when Sinclair was murdered.’

‘Yes,’ said Grant.

'And the information about the car was interesting.'

'The Audi that Campbell stole was dark blue,' said Grant.

'And Baxter's car's dark green,' said Logan.

She turned her chair and looked out of the window into the park across the road. Some young children were playing while their mothers lay on the grass in the warm sunshine. Logan remembered that this time the day before she had been on the beach. A lot had happened since then.

She turned and looked at her watch. It was already three thirty in the afternoon.

'Yes, I think we should talk to Baxter again first,' she said. 'Phone him and invite him along here. Say I'd like to speak to him. Tonight would be best; if not, tomorrow morning.'

There was a box full of papers about Craig Sinclair's murder on her desk. She pulled it towards her. 'I want another look at this information about Craig Sinclair's murder before I talk to Baxter.'

As Grant left, she picked up the first page and started to read.

Chapter 9 *Back to the first murder*

Craig Sinclair's body had been discovered in the early hours of the morning at the back of a factory in Beaverhall Road in the Broughton area of Edinburgh. One of the factory workers found it when he went outside to have a cigarette. Someone had shot Sinclair and then taken his body to the factory and left it there.

Logan thought it might be useful to see where this had happened. She tried to remember if she had ever been to Beaverhall Road but thought she probably hadn't.

Fifteen minutes later she was there. Beaverhall Road was a small street off Broughton Road. There were some old flats and a car park on the right hand side of the street. On the left were some big buildings – factories and offices. At the end of the road was a large empty area, where the Powderhall Stadium had once been. Logan left her car outside the last block of flats on the right hand side and walked up the street. It was empty. The fish and chip shop on the corner was closed. There was nobody around.

She walked back up the street to her car. Opening the car door, she took out the police record and looked at the photographs of Sinclair's body. She looked round the street and worked out where his body had been found. Had the murderer known that the factories worked day and night? Maybe he or she had thought that no-one would find the body until the next morning.

Just then she heard a noise behind her. An old man was

walking across the empty area behind her. He was wearing an old jacket and grey trousers, which looked as if he had slept in them. As he came towards her, there was a strong smell of whisky.

'All right, hen?' he asked. Some Scots people call women 'hen' if they don't know their name. Logan didn't like it much but it was better than 'love'. Just.

'All right,' she replied.

Moving slowly from side to side, the old man stood in front of her. Suddenly he looked hard at her and then he stood up straight. 'You'll be the police, then,' he said.

'That's right,' said Logan. 'And you are . . . ?'

'Angus MacLeod, at your service, madam,' said the old man, touching the right side of his head with his first finger and then pointing it at Logan. 'You can call me Gus.'

Logan smiled. The old man had clearly drunk too much but he wasn't dangerous.

'Where do you live, Gus?' asked Logan in a friendly way.

'Here and there. Under the stars. I'm a free man in a free world,' said Gus, throwing his arms wide open.

Logan laughed a little. 'Do you come round here often?' she asked.

'Oh yes,' said Gus slowly and carefully. 'I've been coming round here for a long time. Since before they knocked the stadium down.' And he looked back at where the stadium had been and then turned back to Logan. 'Since before you joined the police, I should think too,' he said, looking her up and down. 'And since before they found the body over there,' he said, and pointed between the two factories. 'But I didn't come back for some time after that. That was a bad business. A bad business.'

'You were here then?' asked Logan.

'Oh yes,' said MacLeod, 'but I didn't come back for a long time. It was a bad business.' MacLeod looked unhappy at remembering the murder and, as he spoke, he took a half bottle of whisky out of his pocket, took off the top and had a drink.

'I mean, were you actually here on the night of the murder, Gus?' asked Logan.

'Oh yes,' said MacLeod.

'So did the police talk to you?' asked Logan.

'No. No. I went away. It was a bad business. Nothing to do with me.'

'But did you see anything that night?' asked Logan.

'Oh, yes,' said MacLeod. His voice was clearer now. 'I saw him.'

'You saw the body?' said Logan. She couldn't believe her luck in finding this old man.

'I saw the body,' said MacLeod. 'And I saw him too.'

'Who too?' asked Logan, trying to understand what the old man was talking about.

'I saw the body,' said MacLeod slowly, as if talking to a child, 'and I saw him too. The man who brought the body.'

Logan could feel her breathing getting quicker.

'You mean, you saw the man who left the body over there?'

MacLeod looked at her as if she was stupid.

Logan knew she had a problem. She should take MacLeod straight to London Road for questioning. She should also be really angry with him for not giving information to the police. But people like Gus, people who lived on the street and drank too much, could be difficult.

He might tell her something. But he might not. She could not make him talk. And if he did talk, it would not be easy to know if he was telling the truth or even if he knew what the truth was. If he gave her information that actually was important, she would have to be careful how she used it. A good lawyer could make someone like Gus seem completely mad. She decided to talk to Gus now. Somehow she felt he would not like the London Road police station.

'Tell me about him,' said Logan.

'Well,' said MacLeod, helping himself to another small drink, 'I'd be very happy to tell you.' And he said nothing more but just looked at Logan with a smile on his face.

Logan found a ten-pound note in her pocket and gave it to the old man.

'Now that's very kind of you,' he said. 'Well, it was the middle of the night and this car stopped just about here.' And he pointed to a place near where they were standing. 'A big man got out, opened the back door of the car on the other side, took something out and carried it over there.'

'What was the man like?' asked Logan.

'Big,' said MacLeod. 'Tall.'

'What was he wearing?' asked Logan.

'A suit,' said MacLeod. 'Perhaps. It was dark. The street lights were on but it was still quite dark.'

'What sort of car was it?' asked Logan.

'Big,' said MacLeod. 'Four wheels and four doors.' And he started laughing. However, when he saw the look on Logan's face he stopped.

'Colour?' asked Logan.

'I don't know, hen. It was the middle of the night. It looked as if it was a dark colour.'

'Anything else,' asked Logan. 'Think carefully. Did you see the car number?'

MacLeod started laughing again at the thought that he might have remembered the car number. But then he stopped laughing and looked at Logan. He took another drink from his bottle. He seemed to be thinking hard.

'Actually,' he spoke clearly and looked her straight in the eye, 'I don't remember the car number, but I seem to have an idea in my head it was an unusual one. You know, like JB 007 or GUS 1 or something like that.'

'Are you sure about that?' asked Logan.

'Absolutely,' said MacLeod, his voice becoming a little unclear again. Then he looked at her as if deciding he had spent enough time with the police for now. 'And now,' he continued, 'if you will excuse me, it has been nice talking to you but I have important things to do.'

He turned and, singing quietly to himself, started walking up the street in a more or less straight line.

Logan stood by her car and watched MacLeod. He seemed to drink too much and he probably believed what he had told her. But should she believe him? No-one else would. But actually she thought she did. It was interesting information and she needed time to think about it.

Chapter 10 *Catching a murderer*

Logan got back to the London Road police station at five o'clock and found a message on her desk. The fingerprint on the envelope in Morag's pocket was not the same as any of the fingerprints in the police records. Logan thought about this. It was not what she had expected. Not what she had expected at all.

At that moment Sergeant Grant put his head round the door.

'Good news,' he said. 'The divers found a knife in St Margaret's Loch. It was on the bottom of the loch inside a plastic bag full of stones. The scientists have got it now.'

'That's great,' said Logan, 'but we'll have to wait and see if it's the knife that killed Morag Mackenzie.'

'They'll let us know as soon as possible,' he told Logan. 'And Baxter's in Glasgow at the moment. He'll be back in Edinburgh first thing in the morning and he'll be here at nine thirty.'

'Thanks, Grant,' said Logan. 'Listen,' she went on. 'A couple of things: first, I'd like to see Robert Baxter's criminal record.'

'He hasn't got one, madam,' said Grant.

'But you told me about the time he was caught with the handbag,' said Logan, surprised.

'Yes, but he was only fifteen or sixteen at the time. He didn't get a criminal record. The officer who caught Baxter just told him that if he did it again, he'd be in a lot of trouble. He thought that would be enough.'

'Well, that explains why we don't have his fingerprints,' said Logan. 'Now there's just one other thing I'd like you to do before you go home.' And she explained what she wanted.

Then, when Grant had gone, she picked up her bag and went home.

* * *

Logan's flat was in Leith, an area in the north of Edinburgh, by the sea. Leith had once been a busy place with a lot of ships going in and out every day. Now, however, it was a quieter place, and many of the old buildings were flats for the young single people of Edinburgh. Logan lay on the sofa in her living room, listening to Capercaillie, her favourite Scottish band, on the CD player.

As she lay there she thought about all the facts that she had discovered. They were like the different pieces of a jigsaw puzzle – the game where you make a picture out of all the little pieces. You can only put the pieces together one way to make a picture. If you put them together the wrong way, you find that you can't use some of the pieces. She lay there for hours trying to find the right way to make a complete picture.

By midnight she had finally put an almost complete picture together. There were still a couple of pieces that she couldn't quite put in. However, she hoped her conversation with Robert Baxter the next morning would take care of those problems.

*   *   *

The next morning, Logan sat at her desk with a cup of hot black coffee, reading the message that Grant had left after his visit to Brown's flat.

There was a knock at her door and Sergeant Grant came in.

'Morning, Grant. Thanks for this,' she said, waving the piece of paper at him and then putting it in her pocket.

'I've got news from the scientists about the knife,' he said, sounding pleased. 'We're in luck.'

'Go on,' said Logan.

'It's the knife which killed Morag – her blood is on it.'

'OK. That's a good start,' said Logan.

'And the knife was probably in a plastic bag with stones because the handle is wooden. The murderer must have been worried that it wouldn't stay at the bottom of the loch,' Grant said.

Logan said nothing, realising that there was more information to come.

'Because the knife was in a plastic bag, very little water got in and the scientists have been able to find some fingerprints on it.'

'Great,' said Logan.

'And one of the fingerprints is the same as the fingerprint on the envelope.'

Logan banged the top of her desk with her hand. 'Excellent,' she said. 'Now is Baxter here yet?'

'Yes,' said Grant. 'I've put him in the room you asked for and given him a cup of coffee. But I still don't understand. We're sure the murderer knew Morag and we know the murderer was left-handed. Campbell and Brown both knew her and they're both left-handed. Baxter may be the main man but we're not sure. He says he never knew her. And he's right-handed. We've seen him playing tennis.'

Logan just smiled at him.

'You haven't got a packet of cigarettes, have you?' she asked.

Grant gave her a surprised look. Logan didn't smoke.

'Sure,' he said, and gave her a packet of cigarettes and a box of matches which he took from his pocket.

'Thanks. I'll let you have them back later,' she said, still smiling. 'OK. Let's go and talk to Baxter.'

Logan opened the door and walked into the room where Robert Baxter was sitting. The usual rooms where the police talked to people were small with only a little furniture: three or four hard chairs and a table, but nothing else. Logan had chosen a different, more comfortable, room. It was bigger too and it would be easier for Baxter to move. Logan wanted him to be able to move. She wanted him to be able to move his arms. There were comfortable chairs and a low table with magazines. There was a coffee machine in the corner and pictures on the wall. Baxter was sitting in a chair reading a magazine. He put it down as Logan and Grant came in.

'Good morning, Mr Baxter,' said Logan. 'Thank you very much for coming here this morning. There are just a couple of things I'd like to get clear.'

'That's all right, Inspector,' said Baxter, watching Logan carefully, 'but I did answer all your questions last time. I'll do my best to help you today but after that I would be happier if you left me alone.'

'Fine,' said Logan. 'Cigarette?' As she spoke, she took

Grant's packet of cigarettes out of her pocket and threw it lazily towards Baxter. The packet turned over in the air and fell towards the left arm of Baxter's chair. Baxter's left hand shot out to catch it. He took a cigarette out of the packet, put it in his mouth and threw the packet back with his left hand.

'Thanks,' he said.

Logan threw him the matches. Again they fell towards the left arm of the chair. Again Baxter caught with his left hand. He lit his cigarette and threw the matches back easily with his left hand.

Logan looked at Grant. Grant smiled. Baxter saw the smile.

'What's going on?' he asked, looking from Logan to Grant and back.

'You're not bad at sport, are you?' said Logan.

'So what?' asked Baxter. He was beginning to realise something was wrong.

'What sports do you play, as well as tennis?' asked Logan.

'Football, squash. I've also played rugby and cricket. What's all this about?'

'And like many good sportspeople,' continued Logan, 'you're good with both hands, aren't you? You're not completely right-handed; you're very good with your left hand too.'

'So?' asked Baxter, angrily.

'So,' said Logan, 'the person who murdered Morag Mackenzie was left-handed.'

'You're mad,' said Baxter. 'You're completely mad. I've told you I've never heard of her.'

Logan pulled a piece of paper out of her pocket and looked at it.

'Have you got a mobile phone?' she asked Baxter.

'Of course,' he replied.

'And is this the number?' Logan read a number from the piece of paper.

'Yes,' said Baxter, looking at it. 'But you could easily get that information.' He was beginning to look more worried.

'Yes,' said Logan. 'It was easy to get. Last night Sergeant Grant got the phone records for Morag Mackenzie's flat. She called your number at about midday on the day she was murdered.'

'She could have got my number from anyone,' he said, looking round the room as if he wanted to find a way out.

Logan continued: 'We've got an envelope which we found in Morag's pocket. It's got her name on and it will be interesting to compare the handwriting on the envelope with your handwriting. And there's a fingerprint on it too.'

Baxter's face started to go red.

'So perhaps I did know her. But that doesn't mean I killed her. You don't know that.'

'But we will know very soon, Mr Baxter,' said Logan seriously. 'You see, we've also found the knife that killed Morag Mackenzie and there are fingerprints on that too.'

'You don't know they're my fingerprints,' said Baxter.

'No, we don't,' said Logan, 'but I think we'll find they are. And you haven't told us the truth about you and Morag Mackenzie. You certainly knew her, and you spoke to her just before she was murdered. We know enough now to take your fingerprints. We can then compare them with those that we have found on the envelope and the knife.'

Baxter's head fell forward into his hands.

Logan turned to Grant. 'Take Mr Baxter's fingerprints and organise a search of the sports centre on Corstorphine Road and Mr Baxter's home. We're looking for clothes with a lot of blood on them. I don't think we'll find them but, you never know, we may get lucky.'

Chapter 11 *The last pieces of the puzzle*

Grant brought in some fingerprint ink and paper and took Baxter's fingerprints. He left the room for a short time to take them to the scientists. When he returned, Logan started talking to Baxter again.

'OK,' she said. 'Let's go right back to the start, to the murder of Craig Sinclair.'

Baxter's eyes looked empty. He shook his head slowly from side to side, as if he could not believe what was happening.

'Yes,' Logan went on, 'I've been looking at that murder too. And, actually, I've had some good luck. I found a man who saw you leaving Sinclair's body in Beaverhall Road. He described you and your car and he even told me your car number. You shouldn't have such an easy number to remember.'

She didn't tell Baxter that Gus MacLeod couldn't actually remember the number and that anyway nobody would ever believe him. It was enough that Baxter believed that she had found him. Logan was now quiet. If Baxter believed that she knew everything, he might tell her the things she didn't know. Grant and Logan watched him thinking. Baxter opened his mouth and started to speak a couple of times but then stopped. It was as if he could not quite decide what to say. Would he still say he knew nothing, although the police already knew so much? Or would he tell the truth? Finally he spoke.

'Sinclair tried to steal some money from me. Actually he did steal it. And then he started telling everyone about it: "I've got Bags's money. Bags is no good any more. I'm the boss now." So I had to do something. I got my money back and I made sure no-one else would try to steal from me and everyone knew I was still the main man.'

'And you made us think that Campbell killed Sinclair,' said Grant.

'Why not?' Baxter's shoulders went up and down. 'I knew Campbell a little and I didn't like him much. He and Sinclair worked together sometimes. I thought they might have worked together getting my money. I thought it was a clever idea to make both of them disappear at the same time. And I knew that if Campbell went to prison for Sinclair's murder, I wouldn't.'

'So you put the gun in his flat?' said Logan.

'Yes. I found a box under the sink in the kitchen. I just put the gun in the box. It was his box. It had his fingerprints on it.'

'How did you get into his flat?' asked Logan.

'It was easy,' said Baxter. 'I've had a lot of practice getting into houses without breaking any glass.'

Logan thought for a moment and then continued: 'And what about Morag?'

'She did things for me from time to time. She was happy to tell the police that she'd seen Campbell with Sinclair that night. I paid her well for it. I continued to give her bits of work so I could make sure she stayed quiet.'

'And everything was fine until Campbell escaped,' said Logan.

'Morag rang and told me about it. She'd seen it on the

news. She was worried that Campbell would come and see her. She said she wanted to meet me. To talk about it.'

Logan said nothing. Baxter had stopped talking and was looking at the top of the table. Finally he looked up.

'The stupid woman wanted more money. Campbell escaped and the stupid, stupid woman thought it was a great chance to ask for some more money to keep her quiet. Well, she was right. She's quiet now.'

Baxter sat back in his chair, his hands on his knees. His face was now white, his eyes wide, as he realised his world had just crashed in the most terrible way. He looked at Logan and said no more.

* * *

At five o'clock Logan was standing in her office, looking out of the window and deciding that it was time to go home. There was a light knock and the door opened. Tam MacDonald came in, shutting the door behind him.

'I hear it's all over,' he said, walking across the room to stand beside her.

'Yes,' she said. 'Robert Baxter killed Morag Mackenzie. And seven years ago he killed Craig Sinclair.'

'I know. I met Sergeant Grant as I came in,' Tam said. He turned to look at her. 'The usual excellent work by Jenny Logan.' He smiled but he could see that she was still serious.

'Thanks,' she said, 'but I'm sure that Ronnie Campbell wishes the Edinburgh Police had done some excellent work seven years ago.'

'What will happen to him?' asked Tam.

'Well, first we have to look at the Sinclair murder again.

That will be easy because Baxter has told us everything. Then Campbell will go free. I don't think we're going to worry too much about his escape from prison or his stealing a car. He's had seven years in prison for something he didn't do.'

'Will he get some money for the time he was in prison?' asked Tam.

'Quite a lot I should think,' said Logan.

'I'd rather be free for seven years than have a lot of money,' Tam said.

'I think Ronnie Campbell would agree with you,' said Logan.

She turned and looked into his eyes. 'Anyway, thanks for your help.' They were good friends so she moved forward and kissed him softly on the lips. His arms came up round her body and he held her to him. After a minute she moved back a little.

'What about that dinner invitation?' he said, smiling.

'I hadn't forgotten,' she said, her hands still on his arms. 'I'm tired. Let's go back to my place first and decide where to eat later.'